BESIDE
HERSELF

Joe Pintauro

357 W 20th St., NY NY 10011
212 627-1055

First printing: April 1990
ISBN: 0-88145-084-7

Book design: Marie Donovan
Word processing: WordMarc Composer Plus
Typographic controls: Xerox Ventura Publisher,
Professional Extension
Typeface: Palatino
Printed on acid-free paper and bound in the USA.

ABOUT THE AUTHOR

Joe Pintauro, a noted poet, essayist, and novelist, is a company playwright at Circle Rep in New York City. Of his play CACCIATORE, *The New York Times* wrote: "He has two considerable strengths: The ability to write sharp, pungent, urban speech and the ability to unleash emotions on a grand scale on the stage."

Frank Rich described his play SNOW ORCHID (published in PLAYS FROM CIRCLE REPERTORY COMPANY, Broadway Play Publishing, 1986) as a "work of operatic vigor, a volcanic uproar of affections and obscenities to rival *Raging Bull*."

His first novel, COLD HANDS, was described by Evan Hunter in *The New York Times Book Review* as "a deceptively simple, hauntingly beautiful book," and singled it out there subsequently as one of the year's finest novels. Mr. Pintauro is currently at work completing a book of short stories, and his third novel.

for
Greg

BESIDE HERSELF was originally presented by Circle Repertory Company, Tanya Berezin, Artistic Director, and Connie L Alexis, Managing Director. The first performance was on 15 October 1989. The cast and creative contributors were:

MARY .... Lois Smith
HARRY .... Edward Seamon
ALEXANDRA .... Melissa Joan Hart
SKIDIE .... Calista Flockhart
VIOLET .... Susan Bruce
AUGIE-JAKE .... William Hurt
BEAR .... Edward Seamon

Director .... John Bishop
Sets .... John Lee Beatty
Costumes .... Ann Emonts
Sound .... Chuck London and Stewart Werner
Music .... Jonathan Brielle
Hair design .... Bobby H. Grayson

Special assistance .... Mark Ramont

CHARACTERS

MARY CANDEE — Fifty-five. A retiring school teacher, accustomed to counselling her high-school students with a gentle ear and a calm regard. But her benign exterior masks a hard anger, and a stubborn denial of her lonely life.

VIOLET — The thirty-five-year-old MARY, at the brink of a new freedom. VIOLET is fully sexual and almost ruthlessly determined to redeem the mistakes and misfortunes of her earlier life. This is MARY in the days when she anticipated a second chance and believed that she could put her life back on track.

SKIDIE — MARY at eighteen, closer to happiness than ever. A college student, editor of the school paper at Skidmore, MARY here is a hot-headed young woman with naive but sincere literary ambitions. She is so securely in love with ROGER CANDEE at this point that her ego is in a seemingly permanent state of triumph.

ALEXANDRA — MARY at eleven, she only wants to be lovely and pleasing. A beautiful child, she trusts that obedience and self-sacrifice will redeem her from life's ills. Her mistake is that she goes too far, allowing grown-ups to abuse her autonomy and to overwhelm her will.

HARRY THE U.P.S. MAN — The angel of death in the monkish dress of a U.P.S. man.

AUGIE-JAKE RAMONA — HARRY's UPS replacement, a
cross-eyed angel of life full of complications that are
often unbargained for. If he casts well with MARY,
sometimes a younger man may be suitable. Let's say
here that he's in his early thirties.

AUGIE-JAKE is a genuine innocent, a soft-hearted man
of childlike tenderness, someone who would help the
downtrodden and anyone suffering depression or
mental anguish because he knows about them
firsthand. Though wonderfully intuitive, he changed
schools too many times in his life to be very well
educated. He is amusingly neurotic and complex,
capable of mustering any necessary lie at will. In his
past he could accept being called 'son' by someone who
did not mean it. He has developed an uncanny knack
for fibbing, for giving responses he feels people want,
but when he is caught at this, he may explode. And just
beneath that anger lies a dark and secret hurt.

THE BEAR — The restless soul of young ROGER CANDEE,
trapped in a black bear.

THE SET

MARY's house is in an almost primeval forest off the coast of New England, nestled in a grove of ancient fern and leggy sassafras trees. Fat-trunked pines and monstrous old elms grow up there above everything like huge umbrellas, dwarfing the forest, making it mossy green and gorgeously shaded there. MARY's house has floors but no walls. It's just a platform in the woods bordered on each side by wide, leaf-strewn paths. (Entrance and exit ways are stage right and left.) And yet an old chandelier hangs over the kitchen table as if from a giant elm, and rosy, incandescent electric lamps are here and there. An old oriental rug is in the living room area, and screens hang separating the porch from the house. A stuffed Bahama turtle—some two feet long or more—rests on the living room floor. It is a fairy tale house, surreal yet natural.

One door, up center stage, is bathroom, closet, and door to the bedrooms of the house. There is a dark, mossy exitway next to this closet, for in this play some characters come and go without using a door. Similar exit ways are possible at other points in the set, seemingly through the woods.

The stage reveals three parts of the house: *Kitchen*—its screen door opens to one of the wooded paths; *living room*—a Victorian chaise on an oriental rug separates it from the kitchen; and a *porch*—two large hanging screens float, separating the porch from the living room. The porch looks onto the other wooded path. All these elements combine to appear as one sweeping space.

As was mentioned above, the walls of the house are just forest trees, which also invade the house, just as MARY's imagination is violating the boundaries of reality. For example, the fridge is before a large oak trunk, and sucklings grow on the inside of the kitchen screen door. Leaves are all over the paths, but leaves have also fallen into the house and are visible in tiny piles around the edges of the house floor. (For the Circle Rep production, John Lee Beatty's set was entirely covered in burgundy rugging to which were stapled multicolored leaves.)

A major highway was built extremely close to MARY's house, separating it from a steamy peat bog across the way. We hear the invasive sounds of trucks whooshing by and sometimes we see warm white air from the peat bog slinking in on MARY's floor, from the porch, from the kitchen door, from the wooded paths. The highway is not visible to the audience, but at night headlights invade as if in search of a criminal. Animals who live in the bog, accustomed to raiding MARY's garbage, are often killed on the highway. We hear screeching brakes at times, and a thud, and then the wailing sounds of wounded animals.

As the world is catching up to this house, MARY's past is catching up to her. Like the cries of the wounded animals, her transgressions are returning to haunt her. Finally, the worst mistake of her life catches up to her in the form of a huge wounded bear who not only bleeds in her kitchen, but speaks to MARY of her crime with a human voice.

ACT ONE

Scene One

(MARY is in darkness on a kitchen step-ladder, looking for something far back and up in her closet. [This closet serves as a bathroom and an entrance to the rest of MARY's house.] Lights come up, revealing a low-lying fog drifting into the house from the porch. A child in a white slip [ALEXANDRA] runs, quick, through the fog, into the house and out. Then lights come up on MARY, who has just had the thought of ALEXANDRA because she found her confirmation dress. Of course, she makes nothing of it—she's just balancing a pile of dusty cartons and looking for the first step down.)

(A freshly baked peach pie is cooling on MARY's kitchen table next to her poetry notebook. We hear the sound of a truck zooming by, so close that the maple leaves of the sucklings press against her screens. The frothy white confirmation dress is popping out of the opened zipper of the garment bag. MARY is singing Paper Moon *to herself:)*

MARY: ...but it wouldn't be make believe if you believed in me. *(She's happy to hear a truck slowing down. Truck door slams.)*

HARRY: *(Knock)* U.P.S.

MARY: Just come in.

HARRY: U.P.S.

MARY: *(Starting down the ladder with her boxes)* I said come in, Harry.

HARRY: Mrs. Candee?

MARY: I've got my hands all dusty, Harry. *(She brings the boxes forward, laying them near the chaise, next to other boxes that she put out earlier. These boxes contain her old purses, compacts, books, records, junk of the past that will come into play.)*

HARRY: You got a dead raccoon on the highway....

MARY: Yeah. Since yesterday.

HARRY: Pretty flattened out.

MARY: Uh, put the package anywhere. It's my fireproof kitchen curtains from Sears. Forgive the mess. My first September not back to teaching so I'm cleaning out my closets.

HARRY: I don't have no package, Ma'am. The storm last night....

MARY: *(Appreciatively)* Aw... you stopped by anyway.

HARRY: Just to say goodbye.

MARY: Noooo.

HARRY: I have to retire. I'm retiring.

MARY: You, too?

HARRY: My wife is going to die. We're pulling the plug tomorrow.

MARY: What? Well, the pie's all cooled. Sit and have a slice.

HARRY: No. I have others to say goodbye to.

MARY: *(Hurt)* Oh, I see. *(Tip)* Well, you sit anyway. *(Cutting his piece of pie)* I decided to be nice to somebody for the first time in years and you're not going to spoil that chance. *(He sinks into a chair before the pie. The man is distraught and looking for comfort. He doesn't want her pie*

or her money.) Are you from the mainland, Harry?
I never asked.

HARRY: I could't live on this dark island. My life is tough enough.

MARY: How old was she?

HARRY: Is.

MARY: I mean...how old is she? Sorry.

HARRY: Forty-six.

MARY: Younger than me. What does she have?

HARRY: A brain tumor.

MARY: Tsk tsk tsk.

HARRY: She's been on life support, lung machine, and I.V. four months. Never made out a living will, you know? I got a court order yesterday. Got it yesterday. She didn't want to live, my wife.

MARY: Who would?

HARRY: Even before she got sick.

MARY: Huh? Sometimes there just isn't anything left.

HARRY: That's crazy.

MARY: What is there?

HARRY: What? To be healthy. To...bake a pie, to greet a friend....

MARY: To give them a tip and say goodbye.

HARRY: Never took a tip in my life. What I'm doin' is passing these out to my customers. *(He hands her a bracelet.)*

MARY: A bracelet?

HARRY: Uh...read. Now I'm not forcin' these on people.

MARY: *(Reads from bracelet)* Do...not...resuscitate.

HARRY: Why suffer needlessly?

MARY: Harry, you've brightened my day. Let me pay you for this. (MARY *goes to canisters and pulls out a roll of bills.*)

HARRY: It's a gift.

MARY: Then this is a gift. (*She hands it to him. He takes it.*)

HARRY: I'm not a beggar. (*Again a truck zooms by, filling the house with noise.* HARRY *awkwardly holds his tip. He hasn't touched the pie.*) My that highway noise comes right in here.

MARY: Have to call the police three times a week to scrape up the run-over animals.

HARRY: It's the moisture from that bog. Smokes up your windshield. I hit a little otter once. I didn't mean to....

MARY: They're run over all day long, over and over. Used to shovel them up to help 'em keep their dignity but I can't bear to look at them anymore. The squirrels.... It's the snakes that just...break your heart, tire marks, ugh...lying limp on your shovel. It's like seeing God in his underwear. Then the turtles...shells crushed and that yellow stuff all over.... (*Suddenly entranced and staring off*) Maybe I'm tired of living here.

HARRY: Now you've brightened my day.

MARY: Touché Harry. (*She starts to laugh.*)

HARRY: What are you laughing at?

MARY: You...you've been delivering here for how long?

HARRY: Twenty years.

MARY: Twenty years. I decide to bake you a pie and you disappear. The kiss of death without the thrill.

HARRY: Well, Mrs. Candee. I enjoyed...the years.

MARY: Goodbye, Harry. Think of me.

Scene Two

(HARRY *leaves and* MARY *picks up her pen and notebook. Suddenly,* SKIDIE *appears onstage, as if she came in from the porch. She's carrying the identical notebook that* MARY *holds.* SKIDIE *sits facing the audience, writing in her notebook and speaking. These words, describing* ALEXANDRA, *will bring her back onstage.*)

SKIDIE: There once was a little girl who could not find the lights of her house. (ALEXANDRA *sneaks into the house.*) She walked through the woods in a white slip glowing like the moon. (ALEXANDRA *sits at the kitchen table, picks up* HARRY'*s untouched fork.*) A very handsome truck driver sees her coming toward him and thinks she is...a motorcycle headlight.... (ALEXANDRA *starts eating* HARRY'*s pie.*)

MARY: (*To whom these appearances are only thoughts hardly worth noticing, she also writes and speaks aloud*) My living will. First.... Lay me out in my violet gown...the one.... (VIOLET *appears out of a dark space next to the closet, startling* MARY.) Oh my God you scared me. You're wearing it.

VIOLET: Who was that creepy man? (VIOLET *goes to the door that* HARRY *used.* MARY *follows her.*)

MARY: Oh this would never fit me...unless they cut it up the back and put it on me like a hospital gown....

VIOLET: (*Recognizing* SKIDIE) Is she still documenting every breath she takes?

MARY: Oh leave her.

VIOLET: *(Rummaging through the cartons she finds a stale pack of cigarettes and a lighter in an old purse.)* Well you might as well tell me. Is he dead?

MARY: Who?

VIOLET: Yes.

MARY: Lionel? Yes he's dead.

VIOLET: Thank God.

MARY: Oh don't say that, that's awful.

VIOLET: What's that river of smoke passin' through your yard? *(She finds a wrinkled pack of Luckies and a lighter.)*

MARY: It's just the warm air that creeps out of the peat bog across the highway.

VIOLET: Looks absolutely prehistoric

MARY: Remember Carol Landis in *One Million B.C?*

VIOLET: With Victor Mature. Sure. She committed suicide. *(Offers a cigarette)* Smoke?

MARY: *(Takes one and looks at it curiously)* They give you cancer you know.

VIOLET: Don't be ridiculous.

MARY: Gave them up twenty years ago. They're stale.

VIOLET: Don't smoke it. *(VIOLET lights up and looks out over the highway toward the bog.)*

MARY: No one knows Carol Landis anymore. You think people will forget Marilyn Monroe?

VIOLET: Something's flattened out on your highway.

MARY: A raccoon. I called the police. Cowards only shovel it back into the bog.

ALEXANDRA: Why do animals try to cross the highway?

MARY: They come to pilfer my garbage.

SKIDIE: Isn't it too wet for raccoons to live in a bog?

MARY: *(To* SKIDIE*)* It's drier than the sewers poor things have to live in. Those developers are chasing them into kingdom come. And not just raccoons...there's large turtles eighteen inches long, and snakes eighteen feet long... *(*SKIDIE *avoids her, repulsed, so* MARY *sits at the table and talks to* ALEXANDRA.*)* ...opossums and beautiful bats at dusk. They take care of my insects.

VIOLET: YOUR insects?

ALEXANDRA: Do you pretend you're Snow White?

MARY: Naaa. I just think of the animals as...company. There's a family of raccoons that jumps from the big tree to my roof and the drummin's so loud I wake up thinking there's big black bears cavorting up there. I put a heavier stone on the garbage can cover so the raccoons couldn't budge it, but then I worried they were going hungry, so I went back to the lighter stone and now I can't fall asleep until I hear the crash of the garbage can cover in the yard. I picture the raccoons using their tiny hands to pick the meat off my fish bones. One night there was a noise in here, and I was afraid to get out of bed, so I fell asleep with goose-bumps and I dreamed of the father bear. He opened my refrigerator, took out a baked apple, sat at the table, and ate it with his legs crossed.

VIOLET: Are there bears around here, too?

MARY: No. We're on an island.

VIOLET: Well bears swim.

MARY: Oh, they don't swim.

VIOLET: Polar bears do.

MARY: Anyway I don't imagine white bears. *(Truck screeches; we hear a soft thud, as if another raccoon is hit.)*

VIOLET: Oh, no.

MARY: *(Dialing. We hear the angelic squeal of the wounded animal.* SKIDIE *runs offstage to see,* ALEXANDRA *follows, carrying the pie dish and fork with her.)* Lucky for those poor animals that I live here. *(Into phone)* Hello? This is Mary Candee again. I want to speak to the chief myself this time. *(Pause)* The problem is that the dead thing's still there and now something else has just been hit. *(Pause; she hangs up.)* Cowards. *(The squealing stops as the animal dies.)*

VIOLET: *(Fed up with her view of* MARY's *lot)* Why did you buy a house on a murderous highway?

MARY: This was once the deepest woods. I still love this place. From here I see wonders no city can make. I'm well entertained.

VIOLET: By a peat bog?

MARY: When the moon is full the light just explodes in the fog and the ground turns to liquid mercury, and I'll take a piece of pie and go stand right there in my nightgown watching that smoky river writhing across the highway, so alive, you feel sorry for it when a car cuts it in half, and you see each half struggling to find the other, and by and by the severed parts float that way east, beyond the pines, and disappear somewhere way over the bay on their way to Connecticut, like the endless beard of God, dragging behind him over the earth....

VIOLET: Try not to talk so poetically.

MARY: I've had sixteen poems published.

VIOLET: Where?

MARY: *Woman's Day, Cosmopolitan....*

VIOLET: Well, you're not Marianne Moore so straighten up and fly right.

MARY: I don't need you to tell me I'm not Marianne Moore.

VIOLET: Oh, you're pathetic.

MARY: I received an encouraging letter of rejection from *The New Yorker.*

VIOLET: Of rejection?

MARY: Well, I didn't turn to poetry to insult you.

VIOLET: Whose wedding ring are you wearing?

MARY: Lionel's. I...I gained weight around it.

VIOLET: You mean you STAYED with him?

MARY: YOU married him.

VIOLET: You didn't leave him and re-marry or get a...a....

MARY: Baby?

VIOLET: A new husband.

MARY: No new husband.

VIOLET: I'd have rather found you dead than like this....

MARY: That makes me feel just great.

VIOLET: ...stuck here imitating some dottery old lady.

MARY: I am some dottery old lady. (ALEXANDRA *walks in, carrying the plate and fork in triumph.* SKIDIE *enters, behind her.)*

SKIDIE: Where've you been in your slip, Silly?

ALEXANDRA: Nobody can see me in the fog. She should destroy this plate. It says made in Japan.

MARY: Noooo. All that trouble ended 'cause Truman dropped the atom bomb on them.

ALEXANDRA: What's the atom bomb?

MARY: Oh, it's a million bombs condensed into one so fierce it can destroy Corinth, Glen's Falls, Schenectady, and Albany combined.

ALEXANDRA: You're fooling. Say you're fooling. Oh God. Did Japanese people...did they...I mean...die?

MARY: Oh yes. It was a terrible thing.

ALEXANDRA: What if the Japanese take revenge?

MARY: Noooo.

ALEXANDRA: Is that why you moved to this island?

MARY: My being here has nothing to do with the A-bomb. The Japanese are so friendly now.

ALEXANDRA: How—friendly?

MARY: Business friendly.... It's.... The war's about money now. Alllexxxannndraaaah!

SKIDIE: Don't call her that.

MARY: She wants the name Alexandra.
(To ALEXANDRA) And you can have it because I found your confirmation dress way back in my closet....
(Removing the white dress from the garment bag) We'll give this a warm iron....

ALEXANDRA: When do you go to church?

MARY: Ummm. First lookit. You're gonna look like a bride....

ALEXANDRA: You don't go to church. Don't worry.

MARY: I have nothing against it.

ALEXANDRA: I understand. You say prayers at home.

MARY: That I do. I keep in touch.

SKIDIE: She doesn't know it but she isn't going to get the name Alexandra. (ALEXANDRA runs to confront SKIDIE.)

ALEXANDRA: I am too. How dare you? I am TOO.

MARY: Why bring this up now?

SKIDIE: *(To* ALEXANDRA*)* Dad said he'd put you up for adoption if you didn't take the name of his sister.

ALEXANDRA: Mildred? Do I look like a Mildred to you? Good grief! I'm an Alexandra.

SKIDIE: In church when they told you to write the confirming name on the yellow card....

MARY: Shut up.

SKIDIE: ...Aunt Mildred was standing right behind you and you started wetting all down your white stockings.

ALEXANDRA: No. I would never do that.

MARY: That's enough.

SKIDIE: She wrote M-I-L-D-R-E-D. So, she never became who she intended herself to be.

VIOLET: Don't I know it?

ALEXANDRA: *(To* MARY*)* Really? Did I? And I wrote Mildred? Oh no. *(Throws herself on the chair, crying)* Oh no.

MARY: *(To* SKIDIE*)* What did you come here for? To wreak havoc on everything?

SKIDIE: Maybe. *(She sides up to* VIOLET*.)* She clams up whenever I ask about our husband.

VIOLET: Her husband?

SKIDIE: Well, all right, yours. Roger.

VIOLET: I didn't marry Roger Candee. I married Lionel Candee.

SKIDIE: Huh? Are you crazy?

MARY: *(Consoling, distracting* ALEXANDRA*)* Well, when a bishop comes to this island we'll go to a church and we'll do it all over again. (ALEXANDRA *pulls away and makes for the porch.*)

ALEXANDRA: We can't. My catechism says it's an indelible mark.

MARY: That's an old catechism, sweetheart.

SKIDIE: Wait-wait, wait a minute. She said you never married Roger.

MARY: I...married his brother.

SKIDIE: Come off it. You couldn't have married old Lionel Candee. Why, he's the squarest man in Corinth. (MARY *opens a drawer, pulls out a framed wedding photo, and thrusts it at* SKIDIE, *who upon seeing it, recognizes* VIOLET.) Oh this will make me throw up. This will. YOU!

MARY: (*To* VIOLET) You be the one to talk to her.

SKIDIE: This is the most perverted thing. You take that stupid cigarette out of your mouth and explain this.

VIOLET: I don't have to answer to you.

SKIDIE: Why... of all the deceitful, warped... mysteries... would you marry... this poor dull man who worked as a rug salesman at Harvey's? That vapid man. I'd never marry Roger's brother. How would poor Roger feel my marrying his horrible brother? They hated one another. Look, I know Dad doesn't like Roger because he works at the mill, but he's going to put himself through mechanics school and open a garage.... Doesn't he realize that?

VIOLET: Roger worked at the mill till he died.

MARY: No....

SKIDIE: Huh? Till he.... Oh, don't say Roger died. Don't say that. Oh my God....

VIOLET: I'm... sorry.

MARY: They all died, Roger and Lionel. A lot of time has gone by.

SKIDIE: Oh, let me out of here. Don't touch me you two. Get away. How did Roger die?

VIOLET: *(MARY and VIOLET look at one another. VIOLET decides to lie.)* Of pneumonia. *(MARY goes along with the lie.)*

SKIDIE: Pneumonia? Oh my poor boyfriend. How old was he?

VIOLET: Younger than me.

SKIDIE: Is this true? Dear God. Oh, I am afraid.... Oh my head will explode. I'm afraid it really will.

MARY: Come...come here. *(They ignore her invitation.)* I'm so very sorry. *(ALEXANDRA comes in from the porch, where she has been drawing in SKIDIE's pad. She runs to VIOLET.)*

ALEXANDRA: Look what I drew.

VIOLET: That's nice. *(ALEXANDRA runs to SKIDIE.)*

SKIDIE: Nice. *(ALEXANDRA runs to MARY.)*

MARY: What is that?

ALEXANDRA: The papa bear eating your baked apple at the kitchen table with his legs crossed.

SKIDIE: *(Approaching VIOLET)* I...I didn't understand why...you married Lionel. I was hard on you.

VIOLET: Roger wasn't dead when I married Lionel.

SKIDIE: What? Then why'd you marry him?

VIOLET: Your next year, junior year, Roger took Joanna Schweeres out on a double date with Cliff Brandeis and Joanna got pregnant.

SKIDIE: That's disgusting! Joanna Schweeres? I will die of humiliation!

VIOLET: Roger married Joanna that summer.

SKIDIE: Did I graduate?

MARY: Yes. And you went far.

SKIDIE: To Paris?

VIOLET: To Rochester.

SKIDIE: Doing what?

MARY: You taught high school for three years.

SKIDIE: A teacher? How embarrassing.

MARY: How do you intend to make a living?

SKIDIE: Writing short stories, of course. *(To* VIOLET*)* Weren't there any nice boys in Rochester? *(*VIOLET *turns away.* MARY *looks after* VIOLET *sympathetically.)*

MARY: She couldn't.... She just couldn't....

SKIDIE: ...stop loving Roger.

VIOLET: (I couldn't) stop being nauseated by the mere thought of him.

MARY: And then one night she chaperoned the senior prom and they started playing...it's cherry pink and apple blossom white....

VIOLET: I walked out to the middle of the baseball field behind the school and looked up to the stars.

MARY: *(*MARY *and* VIOLET *touch their bellies as if in a desire for pregnancy.)* And I thought...my children would be the same....

VIOLET: Time to go home.... *(Overlap)*

MARY: ...so why not Lionel? *(Overlap)*

VIOLET: Why not Lionel?

ALEXANDRA: *(Running in from the porch)* Oh look... what's out there? *(Suddenly, the red flashing lights of the police car invade the house. SFX: sharp, routine police radio talk.)*

MARY: Come here. Don't look.

SKIDIE: What're they doing?

VIOLET: Scraping up a dead animal.

ALEXANDRA: Where are they taking him?

MARY: They're only shoveling him back into the bog so he can be with his friends who loved him.

SKIDIE: Poor thing.

MARY: *(Holding both* SKIDIE *and* ALEXANDRA, *consolingly)* Shhhh. Shall we call it a day all? And go to sleep? We're so tired. Let's give in. Let's lie down now. How I love having you all with me. It's so satisfying.

(Music. Lights go down. They drift toward the darker recesses of the house and disappear, all except VIOLET, *who lights a cigarette and goes off on the porch.* ALEXANDRA *sneaks out and under a rosy light pulls* MARY's *bridal shoes out of one carton and her wedding gown out of another, then proceeds to put on the wedding dress and to march off in grand style to the porch.* VIOLET *is gone and reappears in the changing light—morning light—wearing yet another violet dress.*

Scene Three

MARY: What was Lionel's gripe with that dress anyway? Did he say it was too pretty?

VIOLET: I bought it for his boss's wedding. He accused me of trying to outshine the bride. He'd get afraid if I looked too good in something. Afraid he couldn't live up.

MARY: Well, he couldn't. (SKIDIE *screams and runs in from outside, wearing a black dress that is too large and a black hat with mourning veil and black gloves.* MARY, *seeing her, screams too.*) That's...that's the hat I wore to Lionel's funeral. Take that off. Where'd you get these clothes? (SKIDIE *throws off the hat and gloves and madly searches the boxes for her compact, which she finds and takes to the kitchen table, where she starts frantically making herself over.*)

SKIDIE: I was wearing them in mourning for Roger but I don't need them anymore because he's alive. I just saw him. Roger—oh, you must believe me. I did.

MARY: I'm putting my head in the oven. I mean it.

SKIDIE: I just saw Roger driving a shiny brown truck. He was in a...a brown uniform...with a....

MARY: Oh that's the new U.P.S. man.

SKIDIE: No. Roger! Roger's face...he was Roger all grown up, his very very self. I swear to you.
(*To* VIOLET) You. You'd recognize him. Look! (*She pulls* VIOLET *to the screen door.*)

VIOLET: Is that the truck?

SKIDIE: Yes.

VIOLET: Oh my God that man does look...my God, he is Roger. It's Roger! (VIOLET *grabs the compact.*)

VIOLET/SKIDIE/MARY: (*Overlap*) My hair!

MARY: He won't see you.

SKIDIE: Why not? Of course he will.

VIOLET: No. He can only see her. (*Points to* MARY)

SKIDIE/VIOLET: (*Overlap*) Sweet Jesus!

SKIDIE: Her hair is totally impossible. It's grey.
(*They surround* MARY *with a flurry of activity.*)

MARY: Mind your own business about my hair.

VIOLET: *(On her knees, forcing the slippers off* MARY's *feet)* Hide these awful slippers.

SKIDIE: My God take off this apron. *(*SKIDIE *rips the apron off her.)*

VIOLET: Get her that pretty one.

MARY: Stop. Now hold it there.... *(*MARY *fixes her hair as* SKIDIE *ties the pretty apron tightly around the sagging dress, lifting it over the knee.* VIOLET *has shaken* MARY's *slippers off and is trying to stick* MARY's *feet into the old white bridal shoes that* ALEXANDRA *took out of the box earlier, and that happen to be standing right next to* MARY.)*

VIOLET: Put these shoes on.

MARY: They hurt.

SKIDIE: These clothes. She's such a sad sack.

MARY: The poor man is at the door.

(Enter AUGIE-JAKE*)*

AUGIE-JAKE: U.P.S. Good morning.

MARY: *(Shocked by what appears to be* ROGER CANDEE, MARY *looks up to heaven.)* God, what are you doing to me? You're not the U.P.S. man. You're.... You're.... Roger, aren't you?

AUGIE-JAKE: Uh uh. *(No)* My name's Augie-Jake. Do I smell a peach pie cookin' or somethin'?

MARY: You're not from this island.

AUGIE-JAKE: I'm mainland, uh.... Sign here, please. Your invoice is on the package.

MARY: These are my fireproof kitchen curtains from Sears. *(He hands her a ball-point pen, then lifts the carton so she can sign the invoice.)* What's your name?

AUGIE-JAKE: Augie-Jake. *(He tears off the original, handing her the pink copy.)*

MARY: Is Jake your last name?

AUGIE-JAKE: Last name's Ramona. Italian.

SKIDIE: He's not Italian.

ALEXANDRA: Mama said when we go to the movies stay away from them or we'll come home smelling of garlic.

VIOLET: The pie. The PIE.

MARY: The pie?

AUGIE-JAKE: The pie?

MARY: A piece. It's ready... for you... to have a piece of PIE. Come in.

AUGIE-JAKE: No.... I wasn't hinting or anything. Just smells good. Truck's running.

MARY: A small taste to celebrate your new route. Come along.

(He carries her package into the kitchen. His eyes scan the room, attracted to everything there: her green and yellow stove, her indoor geraniums, her Dutch canisters. VIOLET puts down her cigarettes. AUGIE-JAKE can't see her, but he catches the slight movement of the pack and wonders if he imagined it. MARY sets out a silver-rimmed dessert dish that belonged to her grandmother and cuts him a normal-size piece of pie, then takes her fanciest fork out of the drawer, places it on the dish, and hands it all to him.)

MARY: Sit down.

AUGIE-JAKE: I'll just stand here and eat on the run if you don't mind. Mrs. Candee? That you?

VIOLET: She didn't forge the signature.

MARY: Hush.

AUGIE-JAKE: Hmm? Holy Geez this pie's delicious. Man, Mrs. Uh....

MARY: You can call me Alexandra.

ALEXANDRA: *(Mortified)* Oh, Gooaad. (ALEXANDRA, *who was watching from the chaise, jumps up and marches out of the house, into the woods, still in* MARY's *wedding dress.)*

MARY: My chosen confirmation name.

AUGIE-JAKE: What's your real name?

MARY: What's more real than the name we give ourselves?

AUGIE-JAKE: You're the boss. Hey. *(He gives her a shrug and a smile.)* I have to go. *(He puts aside the empty dish and grins politely.)*

VIOLET: Get him to come back.

SKIDIE: Ask him does he come from Corinth.

MARY: Wait. Now you must make an honest woman out of me and have this other piece of pie and help me.

AUGIE-JAKE: Help you just by having a piece of pie?

MARY: Just sit. Please. *(He sits uncomfortably, unwillingly, as she cuts him another piece.)* I fear I'm being dreadfully flaky and overbearing, but you do remind me of someone from long ago, and it's so like having him here in my kitchen that I'd throw myself off a cliff just to keep you here. Lately it seems as though my whole past is...on fire, and it seems as if I'm going to eventually be consumed by it and suddenly, you appear looking so like him, so much so that it could be his ghost trying to find his way back into my life....

AUGIE-JAKE: *(Suspicious now, and amazed by her flakiness)* I see. You...used fresh peaches.

MARY: Oh, I'd never use canned.

AUGIE-JAKE: Too sweet.

MARY: That's right. They don't cook up right.

AUGIE-JAKE: I never tasted anything like this. What's the pudding in this?

MARY: Crème patisserie.

AUGIE-JAKE: It's mind boggling.

MARY: Well, thank you.

AUGIE-JAKE: You calmin' down?

MARY: Much. Thank you.

AUGIE-JAKE: Do you have visitors...? I mean.... *(SKIDIE and VIOLET fear he sees them and slip off-stage, leaving AUGIE-JAKE and MARY alone.)*

MARY: No. I'm.... Well....

AUGIE-JAKE: No kids of your own?

(Embarrassed, she pretends not to hear the question. To distract him, she peers directly into his eyes.)

MARY: Your eyes. Is one slightly...crossed?

AUGIE-JAKE: Yeah. When I stare, it goes....

MARY: The humanity of real eyes is so...moving. And THAT one *(Comically, she points to it.)* seems so tenderly trying to focus with such innocence that I'm tempted to blurt out my deepest secrets to you.

AUGIE-JAKE: Well, I don't know if I'm up for that. *(Stands and makes to escape)*

MARY: I gave birth twice. But they died.

AUGIE-JAKE: No. Oh, my God. The two of them?

MARY: Premature. Rose Marie, my little girl who I lost... she was six months old when she died.

AUGIE-JAKE: Jesus, Alexandreea. I don't know what to say. *(He consistently calls her "Alexandreea".)*

MARY: Alexandra. Not Alexandria. Anyway, now I feel guilty at your using the name since it's not my real name.

AUGIE-JAKE: You like the name?

MARY: I did. I do.

AUGIE-JAKE: So let it ride. How old would your children be?

MARY: Oh...my goodness, almost as old as you...oh, dear...I'm....

AUGIE-JAKE: What scared you?

MARY: I'm suddenly shocked that you're standing in my kitchen, frankly.

AUGIE-JAKE: But you invited me.

MARY: I'm just surprised that you're so vivid. *(She stands.)*

MARY: Am I a widow...if I left my husband before he died...?

AUGIE-JAKE: You wanna be a widow, be a widow.

MARY: No, I'd rather you saw something other...standing before you.

AUGIE-JAKE: Huh? Nooo. Nooo...I don't see that in front of me.

MARY: No?

AUGIE-JAKE: You're a fine person here. Who am I anyway?

MARY: Who are you?

AUGIE-JAKE: Your new U.P.S. man and you're a nice woman who made me two pieces of pie I just ate.

You're in my stomach and it feels great because I didn't have breakfast. *(Making to leave)*

MARY: No. Don't rush off. No. Please.

AUGIE-JAKE: *(Pause)* Okay, but do you have any milk...uh, Alexandria?

MARY: Oh. Sure. *(He takes vitamins out of his pocket. Pours a number into his hand. She pulls open the fridge, grabs a tall glass, and pours out of the carton.)* I don't have skim. I don't know how you like it...well if it's too much just.... *(She hands him the glass and looks at the vitamins in his palm.)* What are those?

AUGIE-JAKE: B-12. This is what YOU need. *(He flips the vitamins into his mouth and drinks the glass of milk. As he drinks, she stares and remarks.)*

MARY: Good heavens. Oh my, I never saw a grown man drink like that.

AUGIE-JAKE: *(Putting down the glass)* I was thirsty.

MARY: I'd expect you'd have asked for a beer. I should keep some beer and wine in the house.

AUGIE-JAKE: No. No. I can't drink when I'm working.

MARY: Then come by sometime after work and maybe even have a bite of food. What do you like to eat?

AUGIE-JAKE: *(Cautious)* What do you like to cook?

MARY: No. What do you like?

AUGIE-JAKE: What do I like? I like artichokes....

MARY: They're in season right now.

AUGIE-JAKE: Three for eighty-nine.

MARY: You shop for yourself?

AUGIE-JAKE: Of course. Who's gonna shop for me?

MARY: You like the big ones?

AUGIE-JAKE: Expensive. My grandmother used to steam them.

MARY: With bread crumbs?

AUGIE-JAKE: No. Plain. Just with garlic, olive oil, parsley, black pepper, and those pignoli nuts.

MARY: You call that plain?

AUGIE-JAKE: I could eat three or four of them.

MARY: Then I'll cook you some artichokes. Say when.

AUGIE-JAKE: *(He plays along, trying to find a way out.)* Really? When do you want to do it...Tuesday? Say Wednesday? Except...I don't get off till six, you see? Then I have to take the truck...back to the mainland, then ferry back here in my own car.... It's not a great idea.

MARY: Wednesday is fine.

AUGIE-JAKE: Wednesday is FINE? C'mon

MARY: It's perfect.

AUGIE-JAKE: What can I say? I hope nothing comes up.

MARY: Nothing will come up.

(AUGIE-JAKE exits. Lights fade to night. SKIDIE's writing in her notebook, out loud. VIOLET is pacing.)

SKIDIE: That night she paced around just like the first year of her marriage, when she was walking along the wooden sidewalks of Corinth in high heels, so slim the belt just about hung in the loops of her dress, wearin' those navy blue crocheted gloves with bare arms. The men hanging out in front of the barber shop always sent wolf-whistles her way, making her smile, and she'd jump into Dad's robin's-egg blue and cream two-tone Chevy, but when she walked into the house, she found Lionel in the maroon chair with his head to the radio.

VIOLET: Lionel, I swear to you if you don't stop ignoring me I'm leaving.

MARY: Where would you go?

VIOLET: Into the future, where men and women live together without getting married and tenderly hold each other in bed regardless of whether they have sex, where guys brush their teeth with fennel-flavored toothpaste and talk to women about baseball and wear soft sweaters....

MARY: You should have left right then.

(A pale ribbon of fog enters the house and undulates. A brilliant white heavenly light radiates around the edges of the bathroom door. VIOLET *stands, watching the door.)*

SKIDIE: Just before dawn she dreamt that Roger was smoking a cigarette in the bathroom. *(*MARY *sits up.)* Smoke was on the porch, slinking its way inside. She dreamed the door opened and suddenly soap-perfumed skin odors filled the room, and she imagined Roger coming out in his bathrobe. *(The door opens.* AUGIE-JAKE *does not actually appear. Instead, smoke and fog enter the room.)* His wet-combed hair and pale skin glistened in the humidity. He stared out at the bog, his eyes slowly going from window to window, and she sensed the strong aroma of maleness filling her house, calming the walls, making her safe, guarding her sleep. *(*SKIDIE *closes the bathroom door and the light changes.)*

SKIDIE: *(To* VIOLET*)* Did you ever see Roger again?

MARY: Oh no, not you too.

VIOLET: Yes. We had tea in Preuser's Ice Cream Parlor.

SKIDIE: Did he still feel the same way?

VIOLET: Of course he did, but we never....

SKIDIE: So he still loved you—you could tell.

VIOLET: He didn't say so....

SKIDIE: But you could tell. How?

VIOLET: He looked anxious, desirous, sad...in LOVE with me, but we never spoke about it, what happened. Roger had two kids by then.

SKIDIE: Why did you go and marry his stupid brother?

VIOLET: Lionel wanted me...he got nicer....

SKIDIE: Of course the poor jerk wanted you.

VIOLET: Well, no one else appeared who was right.

SKIDIE: After Preuser's did Roger walk you?

VIOLET: Yes.

SKIDIE: He took you to the waterfall...to the iron bench. Did he kiss you?

VIOLET: No.

SKIDIE: Why didn't you let him?

VIOLET: He didn't try.

SKIDIE: Why didn't you kiss him? Why didn't you climb all over him and let him have you?

VIOLET: He was married. Maybe I should have anyway.

MARY: Oh, no. Stop it.

SKIDIE: Augie-Jake is my Roger come looking for me.

VIOLET: He does look like Roger.

MARY: You're both wrong. You're both closer to Roger where you are than where I am, believe me.

VIOLET: I don't care if he's Roger or not. You just get hold of that Augie-Jake.

MARY: What on earth do you mean I get a hold of him?

VIOLET: Get him to like you...be intimate.

MARY: I'm too old for him. Let her make up to him—or you.... You be the one to RELATE to him.

VIOLET: She knows we can't do anything.

MARY: You're thinking in the past. A man isn't the solution to a woman's life anymore.

SKIDIE: That's the most ridiculous statement I ever heard in my life!

MARY: I'm ashamed to think of a young man that way. I can't be sexy anymore.

VIOLET: So in a few years they'll lay you out in a dress torn up the back...and without your having had anything with anybody you loved. Does that make you happy?

MARY: Well...no. I don't remember Roger so much anymore.

SKIDIE: Get him to talk to you. Drop hints.

MARY: Oh, sweet mother. Get away from me.

VIOLET: Suppose she's right. Suppose he is Roger come back to find her.

MARY: That poor, nervous...U.P.S. man is no more Roger Candee than I am Miss America.

VIOLET: I say you're wrong.

MARY: It's too late.

VIOLET: If you're alive then so am I.

MARY: I'm so much older than that boy.

VIOLET: Color your hair. Get a nice shade of lipstick.

MARY: Lipstick is a breeding ground for herpes.

VIOLET: You complained how mother let herself go and now look at you.

MARY: No one sees me anymore.

VIOLET: Augie-Jake sees you.

MARY: This is making me tired. I'm taking a bath.
I'm putting you out of my mind. *(Makes for the bathroom door)*

VIOLET: Not for long.

MARY: We'll see. *(Exits, slamming the door)*

SKIDIE: *(SKIDIE comes down left with her notebook. ALEXANDRA and VIOLET cluster around her as she writes:)* The next day she bought a hair dye that gradually restores the hair to its natural color. She applied it once and it made just the slightest difference in her grey, but on the second application, it darkened her hair and in the mirror, when the light was right, she did seem younger.

END OF ACT ONE

ACT TWO

Scene One

(The three are sitting erect, waiting, dressed for dinner, their hair done similarly. MARY, who is transformed and beautifully dressed, is calmly sweeping. She freezes at the sound of a car engine cutting off. A car door clicks open. When it slams closed, the three gasp and jump up. Soon AUGIE-JAKE appears at the kitchen screen-door. He sees MARY, but not the other three, who crowd around him adoringly.)

MARY: Hello.

AUGIE-JAKE: I came. *(He notices her beautiful clothes.)* I mean...are we steppin' out tonight?

MARY: No. Just wanted an excuse to wear my Chinese jacket.

AUGIE-JAKE: You really look like someone else.

MARY: Well, so do you.

AUGIE-JAKE: *(Removing his jacket, handing it to MARY, who hangs it up. Then she lifts a tray with glasses, ice-bucket, and a bottle of Cold Duck, trying to lead AUGIE-JAKE to a sitting place down left. But he's absorbed by the canisters on the refrigerator.)* Hey, my grandmother had these canisters, with the windmill and the Dutch kids ice-skating, exactly the same.

MARY: Where's your grandmother now?

AUGIE-JAKE: Oh, she still lives up in Niagara Falls. She's not my real grandmother, though.

MARY: I honeymooned at Niagara Falls. *(Taking off for the sitting place.* AUGIE-JAKE *follows* MARY. VIOLET, SKIDIE, *and* ALEXANDRA *follow him in a line.)* The liquor store man introduced me to something called Cold Duck.

AUGIE-JAKE: I'd rather have milk with ice, please.

MARY: Are you serious?

AUGIE-JAKE: Yeah. I like milk with ice. *(*MARY *puts down the tray, leaves* AUGIE-JAKE, *and goes back to the fridge. The others follow her back.* AUGIE-JAKE, *unknowingly, follows them.)*

MARY: *(Opening the fridge and preparing the ice and milk)* Did Roger like milk with ice? *(*VIOLET *and* SKIDIE *shake their heads no.)* Uh...your folks alive?

AUGIE-JAKE: Some are, some aren't.

MARY: Some are, some aren't?

AUGIE-JAKE: Okay, all right, I was a foster kid.

MARY: You didn't look Italian to me.

AUGIE-JAKE: Oh, I'm Italian. My dad's Italian. He adopted me.

MARY: But he wasn't your blood father.

AUGIE-JAKE: So? I've known him all my life though. His wife is my blood mother.

MARY: And what was she?

AUGIE-JAKE: Always sick, you know? My father had to work, so I was fostered out.

MARY: Always sick with what, if you don't mind my asking.

AUGIE-JAKE: Her sickness.

SKIDIE: (AUGIE-JAKE *can only hear* MARY.) Don't be so rude.

MARY: I have to fish for clues.

AUGIE-JAKE: Clues for what?

MARY: Just for...sociable reasons. What... was your mother's sickness?

AUGIE-JAKE: (*Pointing to his temple, blushing between sips of milk*) Mental. (*He puts down the glass.*) I see my father now 'cause the lady he's got now is a good woman and he's cooled out quite a bit.

MARY: So you know Niagara Falls. Isn't that something?

AUGIE-JAKE: Stinks of chemicals.

MARY: I never noticed a stink.

AUGIE-JAKE: There's these chemical plants all up around Niagara.

MARY: Nonsense. People come across the ocean to see the falls. What's the name of the boat that takes you right up to them?

AUGIE-JAKE: Maid of the Mist.

MARY: Is that still operating?

AUGIE-JAKE: Doubt it. That grandmother, she had a picture of that boat in the living room and out her window you could see the real falls. She loved flamingos, that woman.

MARY: She saw flamingos out her window?

AUGIE-JAKE: I didn't say that....

MARY: There were falls in the town I was born in too....

AUGIE-JAKE: What town were you born in?

MARY: Corinth. Upstate.

AUGIE-JAKE: I know Corinth. I lived in Glen's Falls.
(The other three gasp and sit erect.)

MARY: No. You did? Does the name Candee mean
anything to you?

AUGIE-JAKE: Yeah. It's your name.

MARY: Roger Candee?

AUGIE-JAKE: Who was this guy? I told you I'm not
named that.

MARY: Okay. Okay. He was my brother-in-law.

AUGIE-JAKE: Funny how you and me, we're both from
up in Glen's Falls thereabouts.

MARY: Those falls were teeny. I loved them in winter.
I was thrilled to leave Corinth, if you know what I
mean, but I do miss driving to Glen's Falls to see the
falls frozen over. The light was blinding....

AUGIE-JAKE: I wouldn't get out of a car to see ice in any
way, shape, or form. The shorter days in the winter
affects my mind. I take after my mother.

MARY: How?

AUGIE-JAKE: My mind. I'm not ashamed to admit it.
Haven't you ever been depressed?

MARY: Good Lord, me? Never. I'm not giddily happy.
I get sad, I feed the birds. I look after the animals from
the bog across the street. I keep my hands busy and my
mind active.

AUGIE-JAKE: *(Jumps up to look)* A bog? Hey, in Scotland.
A million-year-old dead man was found in a bog, all
preserved. Wasn't that it?

MARY: I...just...see raccoons. Darn things are heavy as
bears at night. They jump on my roof from the trees.

AUGIE-JAKE: Bears on your roof?

MARY: I said...I hear raccoons drumming on the roof. Some weigh forty pounds...so, so I imagine...I imagine....

AUGIE-JAKE: Ever feel like crying?

MARY: I beg your pardon?

AUGIE-JAKE: Ever feel like crying?

MARY: *(Avoidance)* Would you mind...if I kick off my shoes? *(She kicks off her shoes.)* I believe the more one cries, the more one likes it, and in spite of how enjoyable crying admittedly is, I will not pay the price of turning into a red-eyed slush rag for the occasional thrill of grief.

AUGIE-JAKE: That's a new theory.

MARY: Oh shut up and open this. (SKIDIE *and* ALEXANDRA *leave in disgust.* VIOLET *remains.* MARY *hands him the Cold Duck bottle. He pops the cork and pours the bubbly over the rim of her glass She has to go down on her knees to sip it so that he can hand it to her. She sips.)*

MARY: Cold Duck is a little disappointing, isn't it? Oh, well. Here's to setting the clock back, to the winter coming, to the dark lights of the holidays, the reds and blues of the Christmas lights. I'd love to roast a goose.

AUGIE-JAKE: Why don't you?

MARY: I would never take a goose's life for just a meal.

AUGIE-JAKE: I'll help you eat it.

MARY: Well that's different.

AUGIE-JAKE: We have a date for a goose now or am I imagining this?

MARY: Now I really will look forward to the cold.

AUGIE-JAKE: Not me. Give me them daffodils. And then...all of a sudden, it's June and the days are too long.

MARY: Doesn't the extra light help you feel better...mentally?

AUGIE-JAKE: It should get dark at seven o'clock and stay that way all year 'round. What is this sunsets four-thirty in the winter, nine-thirty in the summer? For what? Some factory? Makes me dizzy.

MARY: Oh, be serious.

AUGIE-JAKE: Hey! You think I'm kidding? The spring is good, okay? Then it gets hot and muggy, and just when you get used to this-here ocean of light we're drowning in, they trick you by making the days start getting shorter and the next thing it's Halloween and people are thinking of committing suicide.

MARY: Dear Lord, you mustn't do this to yourself.

AUGIE-JAKE: What am I doing?

MARY: You're being mournful. Come on. We have a duty to be happy.

AUGIE-JAKE: Thanks. Now that we know that the mental hospitals will empty out in ten seconds. People around here start getting drunk from September till March. I only drink milk. What am I supposed to do all winter? Hypnotize myself? (*Suddenly* MARY *has got to get out of there or she will burst out laughing in his face.*)

MARY: ...'Scuse me. (*She grabs the tray and runs to the kitchen, where* VIOLET *meets her and the two bend over almost in pain of not laughing, but they can't hold it back and they break out into loud laughter.*)

MARY: This guy could never be Roger.

AUGIE-JAKE: (*Coming into the kitchen area*) Huh?

MARY: (*Sipping more Cold Duck.* MARY's *disappointment in* AUGIE-JAKE *makes her momentarily destructive.*) There's a woman you should meet....

AUGIE-JAKE: *(Terrified)* Oh, yeah? Where?

MARY: Right here. There.

AUGIE-JAKE: I'm jumpin' in the lake.

MARY: *(To* VIOLET, *who is embarrassed)* Go.
(Pushing VIOLET *toward* AUGIE-JAKE*)* Meet the amazing
Augie-Jake.

AUGIE-JAKE: There's nobody in here.

VIOLET: Stop drinking.

MARY: Oh I am unaccustomed to Cold Duck.

AUGIE-JAKE: It works fast. Is this some joke? *(Interested now,* VIOLET *steps up to* AUGIE-JAKE. *The last time* VIOLET *had seen* ROGER's *face that close was in his coffin. In spite of* AUGIE-JAKE's *oddness, she can't help peering into what seem* ROGER's *living eyes, closer, closer, she approaches. But not seeing* VIOLET, AUGIE-JAKE *moves forward.)*

MARY: Stop! You're face to face with her.

AUGIE-JAKE:*(Sniffing)* I think I smell her.
Oh...yeah...hey! *(Sensual connection occurs between* VIOLET *and* AUGIE-JAKE. MARY *steps in and jealously pushes* VIOLET *out of the way, taking her place.* VIOLET *sadly walks off, disappearing into the darkness near the closet, leaving them entirely alone.)* Hi.

MARY: How old am I?

AUGIE-JAKE: You don't want me to guess.

MARY: What difference long as you feel all right?

AUGIE-JAKE: Exactly.

MARY: I just wanted to share my fantasy with you, that's all. Oh. Of course you think I'm island-crazy.

AUGIE-JAKE: Island-crazy maybe, but I know what real crazy is, believe me. I've had plenty of that with my...mother, and you...you're not crazy.

MARY: The wine.

AUGIE-JAKE: I do the same thing on Coca-Cola.
My mind goes ahead of my mouth and the words get
all scrambled.

MARY: I understood you.

AUGIE-JAKE: I get nervous with people. I almost didn't
come tonight.

MARY: But you would've called.

AUGIE-JAKE: No, I wouldn've. I don't have your
number.

MARY: Well, I'm giving it to you right now. *(Writes)*

AUGIE-JAKE: Don't do that....

MARY: Why? *(She gives it to him. He puts it in his pocket,
pretending he has no intention of throwing it away.)*

AUGIE-JAKE: You're lucky I showed up, you know?
I wasn't gonna come. It's a real compliment to you
maybe. I stand up people quite a bit, really. But once I
break the ice, I'm in solid with the person. It's just
during the first time that it happens.

MARY: What...during the first time?

AUGIE-JAKE: I'll walk out on somebody.

MARY: You mean, in the middle of dinner or something,
you'll walk....

AUGIE-JAKE: I'll say I forgot the gas on in my house or
something, yes.

MARY: You don't plan to....

AUGIE-JAKE: They had people like me on *Donahue*
talking about this. All of a sudden it's like you're
having a heart attack and you don't want to die at the
person's feet, so you get outta there wherever it is, so

you could die somewhere alone... where you won't be embarrassed with someone watching.

MARY: Huh?

AUGIE-JAKE: At first it was if I'd go to like... the mall, or church.

MARY: Is it like fainting?

AUGIE-JAKE: Worse than fainting. It's deep deep ugly. Dying is easier because you can look forward to it ending, you know what I mean? This doesn't end. You stay alive so it can happen a week later. But then they come in your sleep.

MARY: Who?

AUGIE-JAKE: These dying spells.

MARY: How does it... how in your sleep?

AUGIE-JAKE: Okay. You wake up at, say, two a.m., choking, and sometimes the vomit gets stuck here in your trachea, and to breathe, you gotta suck the food into your lungs, and it hurts because you're drowning....

MARY: That's not a dying spell. It sounds like a hiatus hernia, or....

AUGIE-JAKE: I had the operation.

MARY: You did?

AUGIE-JAKE: Scar from here to here. How would you like it if I told you that the operation didn't work?

MARY: No.

AUGIE-JAKE: Still get it once or twice a month.

MARY: My God, when are you going to do something about this?

AUGIE-JAKE: I already went... to the Sleep Center in New York. They kept me forty-eight hours with electric wires in my nostrils, down my throat, into my stomach with this balloon on the end like a Roto-rooter. *(He is becoming hyper-manic, speaking faster with crescendoing volume.)* Then they sandpaper your skin and cement these wires into your hair, your ears, thighs, calves, on your eyes like you were one of these monkeys they sent into space. Then they tell you, "Fall asleep," but you can't 'cause there's a television camera on you with a monitor in your room and you go crazy, 'cause... outside your door is this loud machine, like a newspaper printer makin' noise like a car accident every two seconds, head-on collisions... jug a jung, jug a jung, recording your heartbeat, brain waves, and you feel about as comfortable about sleeping as if somebody is looking up your rectum with a flashlight....

MARY: Stop! You've got to... bring in some wood.

AUGIE-JAKE: What're you talkin' about all of a sudden?

MARY: From the woodpile. So we can have a fire in the living room. Please. I beg you.

AUGIE-JAKE: Uh. Sure. Stay calm.

MARY: And I'll get the food.

(Lights fade on AUGIE-JAKE *and* MARY, *and come up on* VIOLET *and* SKIDIE, *who have wandered in from the porch.* SKIDIE *is writing in her notebook.)*

SKIDIE: He didn't even look like Roger any more. He was just a rude and total stranger in her house — still, she heated up the pot roast and six very large artichokes while he worked fanatically... *(Cross out)* maniacally, laying enough wood for twenty fires. During dinner he talked himself breathless, not even giving her a chance to change the subject. *(To* VIOLET*)* That man never was nor ever will be my Roger.

VIOLET: Yeah, but don't you think he's a helluva good-lookin' guy?

SKIDIE: You can both keep him.

VIOLET: Then why are you writing about him?

SKIDIE: As a writer I'm interested in all forms of life...no matter how low. *(Back to her writing)* After dinner, she threw more logs on the fire and he drank his coffee with his elbows touching his knees as he gazed into the fire. The primitive and calming effect of the fire had taken over the room. The crackling noises seemed to demand silence, and at last the man stopped speaking until the glow had quieted into darkly jeweled embers. *(VIOLET and SKIDIE walk off the porch, into the woods. Lights up on AUGIE-JAKE and MARY having coffee before the fire. Cookies are nearby. MARY reflects SKIDIE's disappointment. Sobered by AUGIE-JAKE's psychological complexity, she entertains him now with a soft, schoolteacher's pity. AUGIE-JAKE feels the pressure of this change.)*

AUGIE-JAKE: I talked too much. I made you squeamish. I'm sorry.

MARY: I enjoyed your talking.

AUGIE-JAKE: I couldn't stop. It's not me, really....

MARY: You seem yourself, almost too much.

AUGIE-JAKE: Only 'cause I'm a thousand times more relaxed than usual. *(Lie)*

MARY: Why wouldn't you be relaxed?

AUGIE-JAKE: I'm not sociable with people. I don't enjoy people.

MARY: Are you enjoying me?

AUGIE-JAKE: I am. Truthfully.

MARY: You don't have to pretend with me.

AUGIE-JAKE: Oh no, you make me comfortable 'cause I can see you're... you're to be trusted. I like the way you live here. I can tell a lot about you from your canisters, this rug...the turtle. I swear.

MARY: Tell me the truth about you.

AUGIE-JAKE: You want more? I'm talking my head off here.

MARY: What do you do after work...or....

AUGIE-JAKE: Watch *Wheel of Fortune*. Rent a movie now and then. I lead a very boring life.

MARY: Boring for you, or according to others?

AUGIE-JAKE: What about people like you and me can't be boring?

MARY: Thanks. I can be fairly interesting given a chance.

AUGIE-JAKE: See what I just did? Insulted you. See what I mean? Okay, let me try to answer. What do I do.... Okay. When I'm alone, I tell myself I'm okay, you know? That I like being alone in the apartment, but the best would be to be with someone and at the same time to be as calm as when I'm alone. I admit it. That would be the max.

MARY: So until you get up the courage to find a girlfriend, you watch movies?

AUGIE-JAKE: Thank God for movies you could say.

MARY: In school...what did you like...say, for example, in English?

AUGIE-JAKE: Here it comes. Go ahead. Finish.

MARY: What do you mean?

AUGIE-JAKE: I am not retarded.

MARY: I didn't dream....

AUGIE-JAKE: I've had intelligent tests and I am not retarded, so don't worry....

MARY: But that's not what I thought.

AUGIE-JAKE: Okay, but it's taken care of if it should pop into your....pop, swhwwt, my teeth are falling out...pop into your head.

MARY: Your teeth are falling out...?

AUGIE-JAKE: Just a matter of speaking, or is it manner? Manner? Geez.

MARY: You didn't mention any of your male relatives.

AUGIE-JAKE: What the hell made you say that for?

MARY: Did you spend most of your time with women?

AUGIE-JAKE: Hey. Lady. These are pretty direct questions for a woman who is supposed to be so polite and respectable.

MARY: I'm sorry.

AUGIE-JAKE: I had a couple of brothers who were hell-bent on killing me. Who wants to remember that?

MARY: They wanted to kill you?

AUGIE-JAKE: How would you feel if a strange boy came into the family all of a sudden and took the attention away from the mother? Things like that.

MARY: And did you conform to their idea of you?

AUGIE-JAKE: There you may have something. I talked about my father, didn't I? The women were good to me, that's all. Why make a pot-roast dinner into a horror show? *(Sip)* Good coffee. *(Pause)* Sometimes if a man dies, you know, some guy I called "Pop" or "Uncle", I'll go to the wake if they call me up, but when a woman dies, I hide out in my room for days. They think I don't care, like, I don't regard her as my family, or I'm holding some grudge, but it's just that I can't stand it. It tears me up and it's not fair....

MARY: What's not?

AUGIE-JAKE: To have all these fake relatives who die, and none of them are even really mine. I had seven mothers. I already went through three mothers' deaths; one mother's an extreme diabetic, an alchoholic sister in jail 'cause she head-on collided with a honeymoon couple in the Catskills, one sister a drug addict and a drunk, and I worry about Debra with AIDS and all. Then the cancer of the breasts, the gall bladders, the pneumonias of the grandmothers. It don't let up.

MARY: You should call them step-relatives. That would make it easier.

AUGIE-JAKE: Excellent comment. Excellent.

MARY: Have a cookie.

AUGIE-JAKE: No, thank you.

MARY: I almost baked an apple pie for dessert, but I thought we'd have too much food.

AUGIE-JAKE: I never turn down apple pie.

MARY: Oh, no. Now I'm sorry.

AUGIE-JAKE: With a wedge of cheddar cheese? That's my heaven.

MARY: Now I feel guilty.

AUGIE-JAKE: Nooooo. Don't be that way. There'll be a time for apple pie again. How do you like that? Alexandria?

MARY: You don't have to....

AUGIE-JAKE: *(Pointing at the turtle)* Has that thing been lookin' at me all this while?

MARY: What thing? Oh, Oscar?

AUGIE-JAKE: He a real turtle?

MARY: Yes. It's one of those giant Bahama sea turtles. It's been dried out somehow. It was in the house when I bought it.

AUGIE-JAKE: Geez, it's big.

MARY: And it's only a baby. I only keep it because I feel sorry for it. It's already lost its life. I can't bring myself to throw it away. They grow to tons.

AUGIE-JAKE: Are those real eyes?

MARY: They're glass.

AUGIE-JAKE: He's lookin' right at me.

MARY: Shall I put it in the closet?

AUGIE-JAKE: No. No. I should be going anyway.

MARY: It's early.

AUGIE-JAKE: I gotta get up for...something. Work! I had fun.

MARY: One day maybe I'll bake that apple pie and cheddar for you.

AUGIE-JAKE: How about tomorrow?

MARY: *(Reluctantly)* Well, if you like...perhaps...but....

AUGIE-JAKE: I was only kidding, Alexandreea.

MARY: You don't have to call me that.

AUGIE-JAKE: No one is forcin' me.

MARY: Well...I'd rather you didn't after all.

AUGIE-JAKE: It's the only name I have for you, right? Or should I call you Mrs. Candee?

MARY: *(A little impatiently)* Oh, call me whatever you like.

AUGIE-JAKE: Hey. You miss a man to cook for, right? You're lonely? So what? *(He moves in close.)*

MARY: No. You're mistaken.

AUGIE-JAKE: I'm sorry I'm not....

MARY: No.

AUGIE-JAKE: ....what you expected. Don't blush now....
(ALEXANDRA, VIOLET, *and* SKIDIE *appear, come to watch
the last moments between the two.* SKIDIE *is reading from her
notes:*)

SKIDIE: She looked at her feet and before she could look
back up she had a sensation of falling forward, but it
was because he was leaning toward her. His face was so
near she could smell his after-shave. And before her
eyes could re-focus his lips had touched her cheek. And
when she lifted her face, his mouth caught hers and she
felt the wetness and the full pressure of his kiss. She
squeezed her eyes closed as if she were being entombed
and she groped for an escape, but the only way out was
through the kiss itself. So, she gave him whatever she
remembered of such a kiss and it worked. She lifted
him out of the dark like a bird, higher and higher,
finally landing on a bright mountain ledge somewhere.

MARY: I'm too old for you.

AUGIE-JAKE: From a helicopter, we're just little moving
dots.

MARY: Oh, that's beautiful.

SKIDIE: Oh brother.

MARY: I do want to see you tomorrow.

AUGIE-JAKE: You will. You will. 'Night...Alex.
(*Exits. Music.* MARY *takes off her earrings and turns out the
lights. She removes her pearls. The women react to his
departure in a way that shows how tenderly they feel, and
how they miss a man in their lives. They start helping one
another to undress for bed. In their slips they let down their
hair and in a trance-like affectation they brush their hair,*

somehow becoming united in the same thought. MARY *puts on her short, Chinese robe and sits in* AUGIE-JAKE's *chair down left, staring at the moon.* SKIDIE *and* ALEXANDRA *kneel, watching* MARY. *Then the bathroom door opens just as before, and steam and an intense white beam of light shoots out and catch* VIOLET, *standing there. This time* AUGIE-JAKE, *as a memory of* ROGER, *emerges, dressed in a bathrobe. He walks to* VIOLET, *kisses her.* VIOLET *holds him and leans on his chest. The others depart slowly into the darkness, watching the two lovers.* MARY *is the last to leave, removing her Chinese robe, staring ecstatically at the two, exiting through the bathroom door and closing it. The* AUGIE-JAKE/ROGER *apparition then takes leave of* VIOLET. *She follows, then stops, letting him disappear beyond the windows and the porch, into the darkness and the mists.)*

Scene Two

(We're in the sunset hour of early evening. Pick-up trucks are on their way home from work. MARY's *been waiting a week for* AUGIE-JAKE *to show up.* ALEXANDRA *is drawing in her book on the rug;* SKIDIE *is in the chaise reading an old* Life *magazine.* MARY's *pretty cotton dress and perky apron seem tired. Her hair, piled in a fifties upsweep, is now falling down. Her lipstick is worn off.* AUGIE-JAKE's *apple pie is on the table, plates, forks, and a pie knife waiting.* VIOLET *is standing at the screens, looking out over the highway. She,* SKIDIE, *and* ALEXANDRA *are dressed for bed.* MARY *decides to taste the pie.)*

SKIDIE: Watch. In the next minute she's gonna cut herself a piece....

ALEXANDRA: Jeepers creepers, take a hint. She should have baked him a garlic pie. Then he'd might 'a shown up. (MARY *puts her piece on a dish and comes down left, talking.)*

MARY: Best best I ever baked. Mnnn. Apples didn't break down and...just the right cinnamon. The others were good. But this crust.... My God, it's moist and crispy at the same time, an impossibility. It's a pastry. It should taste like one but not that it makes your teeth ring. It's a food for God's sake, not a candy. A good apple pie is as satisfying as lamb chops and mashed potatoes, and this pie...embodies all that...perfection.... It's a shame...nobody's gonna know. *(She grabs the kitchen garbage pail, goes to the fridge, opens it, takes out the other pies, dumping them in one at a time.)* Thursday, Friday, Saturday.... *(She picks up the fresh pie from the kitchen table and is about to dump it.)*

VIOLET: Don't.

MARY: You saw him drive right by more than a half-dozen times.

VIOLET: So? It's good food. Why waste it?

MARY: *(Putting the pie in the fridge)* Why waste it. Don't turn on any lights. I'm exhausted.

(MARY angrily turns out the lamp and goes through the door to her bedroom. SKIDIE cuddles on the chaise. Mists creep into the house. The light transforms to midnight. VIOLET paces. We hear trucks racing by on the highway. ALEXANDRA is looking out over the bog and coloring in her book in the chair down left.)

ALEXANDRA: *(To VIOLET)* I'm looking for bears. What are you looking for?

VIOLET: Go to sleep.

(ALEXANDRA cuddles with SKIDIE on the chaise as the noise of passing cars increases along with MARY's tension. The sound of the passing cars seems creepy, crescendoing to a rumble. These vibrations cease sharply when a real truck approaches. The real sound of a real truck approaching gets louder. We hear the truck skid in front of MARY's house, a

thud and the whining of a wounded animal. The truck goes
on. MARY *breaks into the room in her nightgown, turns on*
the lamp and throws on a robe.)

MARY: That was something big that was hit.

ALEXANDRA: But there's nothing out there on the road.

MARY: Come here. (MARY *turns out the light and cuddles*
with ALEXANDRA *and* SKIDIE *on the chaise.* VIOLET *drops*
into a chair trying to sleep. No one notices the bulky form
entering. The invader knocks over a chair, then angrily starts
wrecking the kitchen.) Oh my God! Who's there? What's
happening? (MARY *runs to the kitchen and is shocked to see*
the overturned furniture and a large black BEAR *standing*
there. The BEAR *is wounded mortally, breathing in a*
distressed growl, bleeding all over her floor. Obviously he
was just hit by the truck.) Oh no. Oh my God.

(The BEAR *looks intently at her as* MARY *slowly lifts the*
phone to dial. But the BEAR *is raising its arm as if to speak.*
Finally he speaks in a terrifying, resonant growl—for the soul
trapped inside the BEAR'S *body must use the* BEAR'S
primitive vocal apparatus to shape human speech.)

BEAR: Mmm. Mmmmm. Marrugh. Marrrreee. Haaallp
meee. Aaammm huuurrrt.

MARY: Who are you? You... you're bleeding all over my
kitchen.

BEAR: Why am I bleeding all over your kitchen Mary?

MARY: I don't know.

BEAR: Touch... touch... me.

MARY: I'm calling the police.

BEAR: I never loved anyone but you, Merrreee.

MARY: *(Putting down the phone)* What are you?

BEAR: I... I gave you a topaz ring, and one summer you passed a piece of rock candy from your mouth to mine underwater.

MARY: *(She looks long and hard at the bear.)* Roger.

BEAR: Yesss.

MARY: Roger?

BEAR: Yes Mary.

MARY: Oh, Lord.

BEAR: You married Lionel just to spite me.

MARY: And what'd you do? Killed yourself.

BEAR: I hated life without you Mary.

MARY: So you just ended it? That was a mean way to punish me.

BEAR: I wanted to free you.

MARY: I didn't want to be free.

BEAR: *(He looks at* MARY *intently.)* Then you wasted both our lives. *(The* BEAR *falls down on his fours and leaves.)*

MARY: Roger....

SKIDIE: *(Running after the* BEAR*)*Wait.... Come back. *(Facing* MARY *and* VIOLET*)* You evil things.... You lied. How did Roger kill himself? *(*MARY *takes a kitchen cloth and gets on her knees, wiping up the blood.)*

MARY: Tell her.

VIOLET: He shot himself.

SKIDIE: When?

MARY: Tell her.

VIOLET: On the morning of my wedding.

SKIDIE: You married Lionel out of spite?

MARY: You didn't have to feel the hurt. You don't even know what life is. It can make you crazy.

SKIDIE: Look at you. Don't you know where you are? You're in hell. You're in hell. (SKIDIE *slaps* ROGER's *blood on* MARY's *face.*)

VIOLET: Leave her alone. She paid.

SKIDIE: You.... You tramp. You smoke. You're sex hungry. How could you be so conceited and stupid?

VIOLET: Why didn't Roger drive up to Skidmore and break into your room? He had no backbone.

SKIDIE: You were too prideful and willful and look where it got all of us. Here with Augie-Jake at the hour of our death Amen.

ALEXANDRA: If you don't stop fighting I'll scream.

SKIDIE: And you little weakling.

VIOLET: Don't drag her into this.

SKIDIE: Afraid of a silly aunt. Why didn't you fight for your name?

ALEXANDRA: I did. They were big.

SKIDIE: So what?

ALEXANDRA: And if they threw me out I'd be adopted by worse people. I'm too young to get a job.

SKIDIE: A job? But they wouldn't've thrown you out. You're a kid.

ALEXANDRA: Yes they would have. (ALEXANDRA *goes to a chair and sits with her head bowed. The others stare at her.*)

VIOLET: Once she was all there was. Just her.

SKIDIE: I'm getting out of here. I give up. I'm following Roger into the bog.

ALEXANDRA: *(Perking up)* The bear? Take me with you.

MARY: I'm going with you.

VIOLET: I'm staying.

SKIDIE: You gonna haunt this place like some house spirit? Ye gods!

MARY: But how can you stay?

VIOLET: Who'll know I'm here?

MARY: Exactly. Who'll know you're here?

VIOLET: Augie-Jake.

SKIDIE: You slut....

MARY: He doesn't see you. Without me here how will you even talk to him?

VIOLET: I'll find a way. Augie-Jake is the adventure now.

MARY: I insist you come along with us. You don't choose anymore. I do.

VIOLET: Look at you, acting like you have a life to throw away.

SKIDIE: You don't have to listen to her.

VIOLET: For God's sake, it's your last chance to stop being stubborn and submit to the absolutely intolerable.

SKIDIE: Good Lord. What is the absolutely intolerable?

MARY: To go against everything you were born and bred to be. *(This stops MARY, somehow.)*

SKIDIE: Are you coming? I said, are you coming?

MARY: Can we...wait a day or two?

SKIDIE: Alexandra. Let's go.

ALEXANDRA: I didn't kill anybody.

MARY: Oh, you didn't kill anybody. Here. Wear your veil. Oh, you're a bride. And you.... *(To SKIDIE)*

Take your Mills Brothers album and...here's your *Life* magazine.

ALEXANDRA: Kiss me?

MARY: Oh, I will kiss you. I will, I will, my delicious little darlin'. And you too. *(She reaches for* SKIDIE.*)*

SKIDIE: No. Never.

VIOLET: You brat.

MARY: *(Grabs* SKIDIE's *arm and holds her from running off)* I made mistakes. I took Mildred, my face was never on a book jacket. I didn't marry for love. I gained weight. I'll live with it. You go. Go be the dead princess.

SKIDIE: You'll never understand.... *(They run off.)*

ALEXANDRA: *(Off stage)* Goodbye. Goodbye to both of you. *(*MARY *drops into a chair.)*

MARY: Now what do we do?

VIOLET: I have a feeling the answer is in that book.

MARY: The Sear's Roebuck catalogue?

VIOLET: Now you've got to be smarter and nervier than you've ever been before. Think, Mary. Think hard. *(*MARY *deliberates, then calmly catches on.)*

MARY: Christmas is coming! Now wouldn't Sears have one of those nonflammable Christmas trees somewhere in here? *(*VIOLET *smiles.* MARY *opens the door and both women rush through.)*

Scene Three

(The light transforms to the morning light of a late October day. We hear a truck engine gently churning. MARY *is baking.* VIOLET *runs in from outside.* VIOLET *has updated her clothes and hair.)*

VIOLET: Oh my God. It's his truck.

MARY: Oh, he's only going to drive right by again.

VIOLET: No. He's pulling in. This is it.

MARY: Okay. Don't make me nervous.

VIOLET: Come on. Take this off. *(Old apron.* VIOLET *runs to fridge, grabs her pretty apron and throws it.)* Here. Put this on.

MARY: No apron.

VIOLET: No apron. *(She throws the apron out of sight and grabs* MARY's *good shoes.)* But out of those shoes. *(*MARY *jumps out as* VIOLET *kneels and places the shoes for her to step into.)* Quick.

MARY: These shoes will never feel right. *(*VIOLET *is urgently looking for something.)*

VIOLET: Now.... Where's James Joyce?

MARY: He's where he should be, in the bog with Roger.

VIOLET: Read this right here.

MARY: Is he out of the truck? *(*VIOLET *pushes the book in* MARY's *face.* MARY *reads blandly as she fixes her own hair.)* "Welcome oh life. I go to encounter for the millionth time...."

VIOLET: The reality...

MARY: "...the reality of experience and to..."

VIOLET: Forge.

MARY: "...forge in the smithy of my soul, the uncreated conscience of my race."

VIOLET: Believe it. Get the pie out of the oven.

MARY: It hasn't been in ten minutes.

VIOLET: To hell with it. Let it smell up the house. Take it out.

MARY:*(Removing the half-baked pie from the oven and putting it atop the stove)* That Augie-Jake Ramona I see at my door? Well what...a surprise...indeed.
*(Opening door)*Hello. I mean, hi.

AUGIE-JAKE: Sign at the bottom. *(Hands her the clipboard. She pretends to be able to see without her glasses, and is about to sign upside-down.)*

MARY: Here? *(He takes the clipboard out of her hand and turns it right-side up.)* Oh. *(She signs.)* Well, how've you been, Augie-Jake?

AUGIE-JAKE: Fine, thank you, Ma'am.

MARY: Are you all right?

AUGIE-JAKE: Why wouldn't I be?

MARY: You never came for your pie. I was worried.

AUGIE-JAKE: What pie you talkin' about?

MARY: I promised to bake you an apple pie and you promised to come and eat it. But you must've become busy. I'm sure that was it. It's all right....

AUGIE-JAKE: I been very busy.

MARY: Well, I forgave ya and I hope things have eased up so that now you can.... Actually, that pie's too hot to cut, but it'll be perfect tomorrow. Will you be passin' by tomorrow?

AUGIE-JAKE: Busy tomorrow. *(Turning to leave)*

MARY: *(As if he'd said the opposite)* Well, maybe I'll see you then.

VIOLET: Cut it now.

MARY: Oh? *(She puts her hand over the pie, testing its heat.)* Hold on. This pie's cooled off amazingly. I'm cuttin' you a piece right now.

AUGIE-JAKE: No. Don't you do that Ma'am. Miss.

MARY: I liked when you called me Alexandria.

AUGIE-JAKE: *(Objecting to the pie)* You know I have a supervisor....

MARY: *(Another non sequitur.)* Well! Or you can just call me Alex. Here's a fork. Eat. Eat that.

AUGIE-JAKE: *(Angrily cuts a big piece and puts it into his mouth. Suddenly he stiffens as if struck by lightning.)* It'sss shtill hot.

MARY: Good. Let me get your milk.

AUGIE-JAKE: Now, don't.... Tastes kinda doughy.

MARY: That's a new recipe. Al dente. Is it any good?

AUGIE-JAKE: I like it a little better cooked.

MARY: Well, I'll give up on that recipe then. Blow on it.

AUGIE-JAKE: I gotta go.

MARY: You hold on just a second more here....
(Her heart beats fast, she's unleashed her hurt.)

AUGIE-JAKE: What I do?

MARY: I... waited here for you a whole day, several days, not knowing if you were injured or if....

AUGIE-JAKE: Do I look injured?

MARY: You owe it to a person, at least, to call. You lost my number. Is that it?

AUGIE-JAKE: You gave me your number?

MARY: Oh don't you dare pull this.

AUGIE-JAKE: Look, if you're gonna fight with me, I'm on my way.

MARY: We became friends, Augie-Jake Ramona. Yes. We did. I think I deserve a better explanation than you were busy. If you decided not to be friends, I insist you tell me to my face now.

AUGIE-JAKE: *(Suddenly enraged, pointing a rude finger in her face)* You see? This is why they don't want us to socialize with customers....

MARY: Oh, hogwash, Augie-Jake. You kissed me.

AUGIE-JAKE: What? *(As if it's untrue that he kissed her)* You wanna know what the problem is?

MARY: Oh, this is too much to stand.

AUGIE-JAKE: Do you want to know what the problem is? You have too much of an imagination. Okay? Up here....

MARY: I don't have the patience for this deception.

AUGIE-JAKE: Deception? ME deception? *(He's leaving with her dish.)*

MARY: If you have to lie, you must have a good reason. GIVE ME MY DISH.

AUGIE-JAKE: *(Returns and puts down the dish)* I have a...a girlfriend. Are you satisfied?

MARY: Well, isn't that nice? *(She walks into the sitting area and sits; he follows.)*

AUGIE-JAKE: Excuse me. You misunderstood my intentions. *(Shaking his finger at her)*

MARY: Get your vulgar finger out of my face.

AUGIE-JAKE: It was a big mistake for me to take the chance that you'd get the idea I was interested that way, because I was not interested that way.... Now you're all steamed up. It was only a stupid little kiss to round off the whole night....

MARY: And you tried to make me think I was crazy.

AUGIE-JAKE: I-am-just-trying-to-get-out-of-here. Why couldn't I have a girlfriend?

MARY: You can. That's just what I'm trying to tell you.

AUGIE-JAKE: What the hell you mean?

MARY: I believe that you watch *Wheel of Fortune*, but not that you have a girlfriend, Augie-Jake. I'm sorry.

AUGIE-JAKE: You're off...and I'm gettin' out of here, Mrs. Candee.

MARY: I can help you, Augie-Jake.

AUGIE-JAKE: Help yourself.

MARY: That's what I'm doing. Turn around.

AUGIE-JAKE: See ya....

MARY: Once a week. Look at me.

AUGIE-JAKE: Don't make a fool of yourself.

MARY: I won't die. I promise you, Augie-Jake.

AUGIE-JAKE: *(This stops him.)* What did you say? *(He thinks he's been insulted here because she is using something dark that he told her in confidence, and is slightly enraged. He turns back toward her.)*

MARY: I said I won't die. I won't go crazy. I won't get cancer.

AUGIE-JAKE: *(Laughs with embarrassment)* You think...I'm worried that...you're old, or that you...you're gonna die?

MARY: Well...no.... *(She's lying.)*

AUGIE-JAKE: Then what do you think? That...I'm scared you're like my relatives or somethin'?

MARY: No...nooo. *(Defensively lying)*

AUGIE-JAKE: Then what? *(Very embarrassed and angry now)* What do you mean?

MARY: You liked being here...we...we talked and we, we were tender.

AUGIE-JAKE: Tender? Tender? This is what I get for talkin' to you? Is that it? You throw it up to me that I came here for a meal? That I could've got in a cheap diner? I didn't have to come here....

MARY: Why did you?

AUGIE-JAKE: Huh? Why'd I come? See that?

MARY: I know you have to lie....

AUGIE-JAKE: You're an older woman. Didn't anybody ever tell you that? What am I supposed to do with you? Have kids with you?

MARY: I'm not interested in that.

AUGIE-JAKE: Then what do you want from me? To marry you?

MARY: Why...no....

AUGIE-JAKE: A little kiss and you turned it into an opera of hystorical proportions.

MARY: The kiss had nothing to do with it.

AUGIE-JAKE: Oh, yes it does. The kiss. It means you think you've got some right on me.

MARY: You'll have children some day. *(She says this emotionally, sadly.)* But for now, you need me.

AUGIE-JAKE: Now I'm gonna have kids. *(He talks to her with a lump in his throat that can only mean he feels the opposite of what he pretends.)* You—don't—know—nothing—about me. You talked to me only one time. I don't even hardly remember your last name and you're standing there with the nerve to have a fight with me. Why? 'Cause I KISSED you. Right? That's the whole thing. You own me now.

MARY: Because of a little kiss?

AUGIE-JAKE: It gives you the right to harp on me. How'd that happen? Eh? 'Cause I kissed you. Right? Or else where would you get off even daring to talk to

your U.P.S. man this way? How could you if I didn't...
act casual with you that there night? If it wasn't for that
one night you'd be standing there saying these things to
me and I'd say: Hey, Miss, you got the wrong guy.
Right? You follow me? But now...you're my boss and
my new girlfriend all rolled into one when I just spent
one freakin' night being here once for a dinner that I
came to because I felt sorry for you, and I do have a
girlfriend. What do you think of that?

MARY: I think that's nice.

AUGIE-JAKE: Oh, don't give me that. *(Pause)* Please let
me out of this. Let me go. Please.

MARY: I...ordered a goose.

AUGIE-JAKE: You did?

MARY: And guess what's in that box?

AUGIE-JAKE: A fireproof Christmas tree. It's on the box.

MARY: So?

AUGIE-JAKE: *(Laugh/crying)* I'm joining the Army.

MARY: That's patriotic.

AUGIE-JAKE: Then I'm joining the monks in India where
they shave your head.

MARY: Will you be back by Christmas?

AUGIE-JAKE: If I am, I'll call you.

MARY: You don't have my number.

AUGIE-JAKE: Seven eight five, zero, zero, one one.

MARY: I like you. Don't let our goose die for nothing,
Augie-Jake. I hate the killing of animals for nothing.

AUGIE-JAKE: Don't make me a killer now. You oughta
learn not to laugh at people like you did at me that
night.

MARY: I...laughed? Oh, I was a fool....

AUGIE-JAKE: People do serious damage that way.

MARY: Forgive me. I'm....

AUGIE-JAKE: And no more al dente apple pies and put...that wet lump of dough back in the oven.

MARY: I will. I'm sorry.

AUGIE-JAKE: Yeah sure. *(Exiting. Smiling big.)* Al dente. *(He exits.)*

VIOLET: What's he laughing at? Oh dear he fell. His foot misjudged the truck step.... Good grief, he fell again. He can't stop laughing. Wave to him. Wave. (MARY *waves. The truck pulls out.)*

MARY: What do you think?

VIOLET: Oh, he'll be back.

MARY: Oh I don't know.

VIOLET: Oh, he will. You did awfully well.

MARY: Did I really?

VIOLET: *(Picking up another catalogue)* I couldn't have done better.

MARY: That's true. I don't think you could have.

VIOLET: Look here. Pretty. Holly-shaped napkin rings.

MARY: I have silver ones in the drawer.

VIOLET: Poinsettia tablecloth, twenty-nine ninety-five?

MARY: I like the solid red. I need that, the large roasting pan....

VIOLET: And you don't have to order everything all at once.

MARY: Two orders a week till Christmas ought to do it. *(They both laugh. Reading over* VIOLET's *shoulder.)* I want

those mixing bowls.... Wait.... *(Turns a page or two)*
An ice bucket shaped like an artichoke.

MARY/VIOLET: *(Overlap)* A must!

VIOLET: I'm beginning to like it here.

MARY: Oh, good. *(VIOLET walks off toward the porch and the mists that are forming on the edge of the woods. She tentatively pauses to take a final look at MARY and the place.)*

MARY: Where are you going?

VIOLET: Oh, just for a walk.

MARY: *(Suspicious that VIOLET is slipping away from her permanently, MARY removes her glasses, looks up from the catalogue and speaks to the air.)* Really? Oh, I'm glad. Have a good walk.

VIOLET: So long for now.

MARY: Ta ta.

(Music. Lights fade.)

END OF PLAY